CRASH THE GLASS

"Passionately Pursuing Purpose and Breaking Limits Along the Way!"

CRASH THE GLASS

"Passionately Pursuing Purpose and Breaking Limits Along the Way!"

Marcel D. Fears

EllaMent Publishing

Crash The Glass

Book Cover Design: Typo Nerd Branding
Photography: OEP Video & Photography

DEDICATION

This work is dedicated to my two sons, David Eugene and Tyler Louis. There is no limit; CRASH THE GLASS!

TABLE OF CONTENTS

INTRODUCTION

IF YOU ARE READING THIS BOOK, IT IS because this is your season. Not a random moment. Not a coincidence. This is the season for you to go beyond the invisible limits that have existed in your life and step fully into your breakthrough.

God desires to partner with you in the earth to carry out His good will, the very will He planted deep within your heart long before you ever recognized it as purpose. That is the power of this divine partnership. God already brings everything that is needed to the table. He is not lacking in resources, strategy, or strength. What He is asking for is your yes.

Yes, to His will.

Yes, to His way.

Yes, to the life He designed for you.

There are moments when life makes us feel stuck. I know that feeling personally. Times when it seems like you're spinning your wheels; busy, active, even faithful but making no real forward progress. You're doing all the right things, yet nothing seems to move. In those moments, life has a way of pressing on you until you begin to question yourself. You question your abilities. You question your confidence. You even begin to question your place and purpose. But what if I told you that you already have enough? What if I told you that you are enough? What if I told you that everything you need to fulfill God's purpose for your life is already inside of you?

The issue has never been your potential. The issue has never been your calling. The issue has never been God's power. What if the only missing piece was timing?

What if this is the precise moment, your moment, when purpose begins to unfold in real time? What if this is the season when you finally break through the unseen ceiling above you? The ceiling that has limited your progress, restrained your movement, and kept you just close enough to see what could be, but not close enough to reach it.

This is the moment you crash the glass.

Crashing the glass means breaking through the invisible barriers that have tried to define your limits. It means stepping beyond what has been familiar, comfortable, or expected. It means trusting that God's timing is perfect and that His assignment for your life is still very much alive.

Your journey will not look like anyone else's, and that's by design. You are not running someone else's race. You are running the race that God has uniquely set before you. Your pace, your process, and your path are all intentional.

So, challenge yourself.

Dig deep.

Push beyond where you've been.

Set a new personal best.

This is not the time to shrink back. This is not the time to play it safe. This is your moment to rise, to pursue, and to break through.

Crash the glass.

Are you ready?

Lean in.

Let's go.

CHAPTER 1

CRASH THE GLASS

TODAY, WE CRASH THE GLASS. HAVE you ever been in a place in life where you could clearly see where you were supposed to be, but no matter what you did, you just couldn't get there? You could see the future. You could sense the next level. You knew there was more. Yet every attempt forward felt blocked, delayed, or resisted.

Have you ever felt that no matter how hard you tried, no matter how disciplined you were, or how deeply you believed God, you still could not break through to the next level of your life? If that describes you, you are not alone.

The reality is that many of us find ourselves running in the quicksand of limitation and setback. We are moving; but not advancing. We are busy; but not progressing. Our passion, our drive, and our work ethic often seem to yield empty or inconsistent results. Over time, that tension begins to wear on us. And in those moments, something dangerous can begin to happen. We start questioning ourselves. We question our confidence. We question our faith.

Eventually, we even begin to question the call of God on our lives. The dream that once burned so brightly can begin to feel distant. The vision that once energized us starts to feel heavy. We wrestle internally with thoughts we never imagined entertaining; Is this really worth it? Did I hear God correctly? Should I keep pursuing what once felt so certain?

This internal struggle is often the result of an unseen barrier; a barrier that is real, even though it cannot be touched. That barrier is what many refer to as the glass ceiling.

Traditionally, a glass ceiling is defined as a metaphorical term used to describe an invisible barrier to success, an unofficial but very real restriction that limits advancement, particularly within professional environments. It has often been associated with the obstacles faced by women and minorities, where progress is hindered not by ability, but by unseen resistance. For our purpose, however, we must broaden that definition.

Spiritually speaking, the glass ceiling is anything that restricts us from becoming our maximum in God's Kingdom and fully walking in the purpose He has placed on our lives. It is any limitation (internal or external), that keeps us from fully obeying, fully believing, and fully becoming. The glass ceiling can be fear. It can be doubt. It can be past failure, disappointment, or delay. Sometimes it is the voice of others. Sometimes it is the voice in our own head.

But regardless of what it looks like, its function is always the same: to keep you just close enough to see what God promised, but not close enough to possess it. The good news is this…glass is not permanent. What is invisible can be confronted. What is limiting can be broken. What has resisted you can be overcome.

This chapter marks a turning point. Not just in the pages of this book, but in your perspective. You were not created to live beneath ceilings. You were created to walk in freedom, authority, and purpose. So today, we make a decision. We stop staring at the ceiling. We stop negotiating with limitations. We stop settling for almost, someday, or maybe. Today, we crash the glass. And once it breaks, nothing above you will ever look the same again.

CHAPTER 2

CRASHING THE LIMITS OF TIME

ONE OF THE STRONGEST OPPOSTIONS TO our ability to break through the glass ceiling is not opposition from people, systems, or circumstances; it is the enemy of time. Time has a way of pressing on our faith. It whispers that we are running out. It suggests that we are behind. It convinces us that if God were really going to do it, He would have done it by now. It becomes easy to feel as though there is not enough time left to accomplish what God placed inside of us, or that the process is simply taking too long to produce any tangible results.

However, we must remember this foundational truth: God is not bound by time. Time cannot be, and will never be, God's box. God lives outside of time. He existed before time was created, and He will remain when time is no longer relevant. Therefore, time is never a limitation for Him.

> *"Before the mountains were born, before You gave birth to the earth and the world, from beginning to end, You are God."*
> *Psalm 90:2 (NLT)*

God created time for us. He uses it as a tool in His hand to govern seasons of purpose in our lives. Time is how God develops us, matures us, and positions us for what He has already ordained. The danger comes when we allow our natural senses to determine our destiny. If we are not careful, we will begin to measure our future based on our current condition.

What we see.

What we feel.

What we are experiencing right now.

When that happens, discouragement sets in. It can appear as though we are losing when, in reality, God is working beneath the surface. This is why it is critical that the believer lives by faith. Faith allows us to see beyond the moment and trust the process even when the process is uncomfortable.

In crashing the limits of time, we must understand that there is always a window between our initial point of faith and the manifestation of what we are believing God for. Faith transcends time. Faith is what carries us through the space between what our heart is convinced of and what our eyes can currently see.

I call this space the in-between time.

The in-between time, the space between faith and manifestation, can be some of the most difficult and trying seasons of our lives. This is where doubt attempts to creep in. This is where frustration grows. This is where the temptation to quit or to take matters into our own hands becomes strongest. **Yet I firmly believe that God allows the in-between time on purpose.**

There is a reason that space exists. It is not to punish us. It is not to deny us. It is to prepare us. It is to develop us. It is to mature us so that we are ready to handle what is on the other side of the glass ceiling. I have discovered that some things God allows because they are a necessary part of the process. The process is designed to humble us while, at the same time, preparing us for greater responsibility, greater influence, and greater impact.

"We glory in tribulations also: knowing that tribulation works patience; and patience, experience; and experience, hope. And hope makes not ashamed."
Romans 5:3–5 (KJV)

No matter how it looks you still have the victory.

What you are walking through right now is not wasted. God uses what we go through to prepare us for what is waiting on the other side of the glass. The pressure is shaping you. The delay is strengthening you. The struggle is refining you.

Do not allow anything to stop you now. Purpose is waiting on the other side of that ceiling. This is your moment to pursue. This is your moment to believe. This is your moment to crash the glass.

The Believer's Possibilities

Faith plays an integral role in breaking through the glass ceiling. Scripture reminds us that the righteous must live by faith. If we limit our success to our own abilities, resources, or understanding, we will always fall short. But with God, boundaries are removed, and limits are broken.

"With men this is impossible; but with God all things are possible."
Matthew 19:26 (KJV)

Faith must be put into action. When we step out in faith, we step into another realm; a realm where God's possibilities override human limitations.

Faith in God opens a limitless world of opportunity. Yet many of us have spent years hearing what cannot be done, what did not work for someone else, or what religious tradition says is not possible. In some spaces, salvation and purpose have been reduced to rules, dogma, and past disappointments.

But God is greater than man-made boundaries. He is greater than limited theology. He is greater than failed experiences. He desires a deeper relationship with us, one that is rooted in faith and filled with possibility.

Break your box.

Remove the limits.

And remember with God, all things are possible to those who believe.

CHAPTER 3

Don't Lose It in the Moment

"For which cause we faint not; but though our outward man perish, yet the inward man is renewed day by day. For our light affliction, which is but for a moment, works for us a far more exceeding and eternal weight of glory."
2 Corinthians 4:16–17 (KJV)

ONE OF THE GREATEST LESSONS WE must learn on the journey of purpose is this: the most valuable asset we have is time. You can take my money; I can make more. If I lose my house, I can purchase another one. If my car breaks down, I can save and replace it. But if I waste time, I can never get it back.

That is why what we do with our time matters. Moments matter. Decisions matter. Reactions matter. We live in a world that is governed by time, and yet this truth is what makes God who He is God is not bound by time.

God is not restricted by the parameters and pressures of the clock. He lives outside of time and created it as a tool for us. Time is how God unfolds seasons of purpose in our lives. It is how He develops us, teaches us, and positions us for what is next. Because time is so valuable, we cannot afford to be careless with it.

Love on your family.

Cherish your relationships.

Do what you can for one another.

Some of us have been holding onto frustration, anger, or offense for so long that we no longer even remember how it started. And yet, those unresolved moments continue to steal time, energy, and peace. Some things have to be released when you realize how much moments truly matter.

Every one of us will experience moments of difficulty. Challenges are inevitable. Pressure is unavoidable. But what defines us is how we handle those moments. One positive moment; one God-centered decision; can change the entire course of your life. If we learn to manage moments properly, we begin to understand that there is more ahead. We recognize that what we are experiencing now is not the end of the story. That's why we don't faint. That's why we don't quit. That's why we don't lose it in the moment by making a permanent decision in a temporary situation.

Scripture reminds us that the outward man will perish. Our bodies will grow tired. Our emotions will be tested. But the inward man, the spirit man, can be renewed day by day. And that is where our focus must remain. I want my spirit to stay healthy even when life feels heavy.

Our afflictions are real, but they are temporary. Glory is coming after this. God's anger endures only for a moment, but His favor lasts a lifetime. Weeping may endure for a night, but joy comes in the morning.

Never forget this: the moment is not greater than the promise.

So, hold on. Stay grounded. Guard your spirit. The pressure will pass. The season will shift. And what God has promised will come to pass. The moments matter…don't lose it in the moment.

CHAPTER 4

WHAT IS THIS SEASON

REVEALING IN YOU?

SEASONS HAVE REASONS. EVERY SEASON God creates is intentional, and every season is designed to unfold purpose in your life. Nothing you are experiencing right now is accidental. The season you are in carries instruction, development, and revelation. When we become sensitive to the season we are walking through, we gain clarity on what God is trying to produce in us and through us. Our awareness of the season determines what we are able to accomplish in our God-given space.

> *"He has made everything beautiful in His time; also He has set eternity in the human heart, so that no one can fully comprehend what God has done from beginning to end." Ecclesiastes 3:11 (KJV)*

God planted eternity in the human heart and brings it forth in time.

This scripture teaches us a powerful truth: when God created us from the dust of the ground and breathed the breath of life into us, He did more than give us oxygen; He deposited purpose. Laced within the breath of God is the reason for our existence. God has never created anything without purpose, and that includes you. Ecclesiastes 3:11 reveals that God planted purpose as a seed in our hearts. That seed carries divine intention, destiny, and calling. And while the seed is eternal, its expression is released in time. Everything God has placed in you has an appropriate season for manifestation.

There are times, however, when that purpose feels hidden. Life has a way of layering disappointment, delay, trauma, and uncertainty over the very thing God planted in us. Storms can obscure our vision. Pain can distort our perception. Waiting can make us question what we once believed.

But hear this clearly; purpose has not been removed.

No matter what you have encountered, endured, or survived, purpose is still planted deep within the vault of your heart. It has not expired. It has not been diminished. It has not been stolen. Be encouraged it is still there.

> *"He has planted eternity [a sense of divine purpose] in the human heart… a longing nothing under the sun can satisfy except God."*
> *Ecclesiastes 3:11 (AMP)*

There is divine purpose inside of you that only God can fully reveal. It is going to take God to draw it out, shape it, and release it. And that is exactly what this season is doing. This season is not just passing time it is revealing what God placed inside of you from the very beginning. Purpose is in you. Purpose is developing in you. And purpose will be released through you.

Pay attention to this season. What feels like pressure may actually be preparation. What feels like delay may actually be development. What feels like uncertainty may be God uncovering something deeper within you.

This season is speaking.

This season is shaping.

This season is revealing.

And what God reveals in you now will define how you walk into what comes next.

CHAPTER 5

The Power of Recognition

ONE OF THE TRUTHS I HAVE DISCOVERED throughout my life is this: there will always be forces working against you in an attempt to keep you from walking boldly in your authentic self and fully expressing what you carry.

Those forces show up early. They can appear in moments of insecurity like being an unsure kid in high school, or later in life through the pressure of unfair expectations placed on you by others. Regardless of the season, these forces all share the same goal: to quiet the value, purpose, and light that lives inside of you.

But here is what I have come to understand; there is something valuable in you that the world needs to see. And the sooner you recognize it, the more impactful your life will become.

The Principle of Recognition

The principle of recognition is a powerful concept the Holy Spirit taught me through the lens of my own life experiences. Each of us carries a unique and profound treasure within us, and in many cases, that treasure has yet to be fully discovered.

> *"But we have this treasure in earthen vessels, that the excellency of the power may be of God, and not of us."*
> *2 Corinthians 4:7 (KJV)*

Recognition is not arrogance, it is awareness. When we become fully aware of the potential we carry, we position ourselves to walk in all that God has planned for us. My personal moment of recognition, the moment when the proverbial light came on, was life-changing. The Holy Spirit revealed to me the treasure I had been carrying all along.

What once seemed ordinary to me, God showed me was actually a supernatural expression of His gift flowing through my life for the benefit of others. That revelation shifted everything. Because once I recognized what I had, I could no longer treat it casually. This is the principle of recognition: once I know it, once I am sure of it, I can passionately pursue it. This is the power of recognition.

Once I know what I have, I can walk confidently in it. I can develop it. I can steward it. I can grow it. Recognition removes hesitation and replaces it with boldness.

There are times, however, when we need help identifying what we carry. God, in His wisdom, places spiritual mentors and leaders in our lives, people who are in tune with Him and able to see in us what we may not yet see in ourselves. These relationships are not accidental; they are strategic.

Scripture gives us a powerful example in the relationship between the Apostle Paul and his spiritual son, Timothy. Paul played a critical role in helping Timothy recognize, stir, and walk confidently in his gift.

> *"When I call to remembrance the unfeigned faith that is in thee… wherefore I put thee in remembrance that thou stir up the gift of God, which is in thee… For God hath not given us the spirit of fear; but of power, and of love, and of a sound mind."*
> *2 Timothy 1:5–7 (KJV)*

This passage reminds us that sometimes we need a steady voice, a purposeful push, and loving accountability to help us fully embrace what God has placed inside of us. Recognition is often awakened through relationship.

So do not be fearful. Stir the fire of purpose within you. Walk boldly in what God has entrusted to you. You were never meant to hide your gift. You were created to release it. And when you recognize what you carry, nothing can stop you from becoming all that God has made you to be.

CHAPTER 6

GET UNCOMFORTABLE

IN ORDER TO PASSIONATELY PURSUE purpose, we must be willing to upset our norms and challenge our traditions. Purpose does not coexist comfortably with routine, and growth rarely happens in familiar spaces. The pursuit of purpose is, by nature, uncomfortable.

Jesus is our ultimate example.

He was the son of a carpenter; yet He was God in human flesh. He was the unlikely King who consistently defied expectations and disrupted man-made systems. Jesus did not conform to cultural norms or religious traditions simply because they were accepted. He lived by a higher order; the Kingdom of God.

Jesus spoke of a kingdom that many did not understand. His Kingdom was not of this world. The Kingdom represents God's way of doing things, a divine system through which His will is carried out in the earth. This is why our prayer is, "Thy kingdom come, Thy will be done." To pray that prayer is to invite disruption, stretching, and transformation into our lives.

In Luke chapter 6, we find a powerful example of Jesus intentionally getting uncomfortable, breaking tradition, and upsetting the norm all in the pursuit of purpose.

A Closer Look: Luke 6:6–11

> *"And it came to pass also on another sabbath, that He entered into the synagogue and taught: and there was a man whose right hand was withered."*
> *Luke 6:6 (KJV)*

This moment was loaded with tension. Religious leaders were watching Jesus closely, not to learn from Him, but to accuse Him. Yet Jesus recognized something greater than opposition; He recognized opportunity. There are several key lessons we must take from this passage if we are going to walk fully in God's purpose. **First, Jesus broke tradition on purpose.**

Luke 6:7 shows us that healing on the Sabbath violated religious norms. Jesus knew the rules, but He also knew the heart of God. Application for us: We must be willing to intentionally break what we have always known in order to purposely do what we have never done. Growth demands new obedience.

Second, Jesus understood the backlash He would receive, yet He still chose power over popularity. Luke 6:8 reveals that Jesus was fully aware of the resistance, but He refused to allow fear of reaction to rob Him of obedience.

Purpose often requires us to act boldly even when misunderstanding is guaranteed. **Third, Jesus stretched someone else into a miracle because He refused to be confined by tradition.**

In Luke 6:10, Jesus commands the man with the withered hand to stretch it out. That stretch became the pathway to healing. Here is the revelation: the man already had the potential to be whole. The hand was not missing, it was withered. What it needed was movement.

Fourth, getting uncomfortable is the doorway to restoration. The hand had potential, but potential requires participation. In the same way, you already have what you need. But in order for Jesus to bring it out of you, He has to stretch you. Stretching is uncomfortable. Obedience is uncomfortable. Growth is uncomfortable. But discomfort is not the enemy; stagnation is. You have what it takes. You are carrying what God needs. And the next level of your purpose is waiting on your willingness to stretch.

So don't resist the stretch. Don't retreat into comfort. Don't settle for what's familiar.

Let's get uncomfortable.

CHAPTER 7

STEWARD THE SEASON

"The earth is the Lord's, and the fulness thereof; the world, and they that dwell therein."
Psalm 24:1 (KJV)

THIS SCRIPTURE AFFIRMS A FOUNDATIONAL truth we must never forget: God owns everything. He is the sovereign ruler and master of all creation. Simply put, we own nothing, yet we are entrusted with much. What God gives us, He expects us to manage.

This is the heart of stewardship. God has called us to properly manage what He places in our hands. A steward is one who manages another's property, resources, or affairs with responsibility and intentionality. From the very beginning, stewardship was woven into God's design for humanity.

When God created the heavens and the earth, He then created man and placed him in the Garden of Eden not merely to enjoy it, but to tend it and maintain it. Man was assigned the responsibility to steward what God had created. In the same way, God gives us seasons, windows of time in which we are called to steward His purpose in the earth. Every season comes with opportunity. Every window carries responsibility.

If we are going to crash the glass and experience true breakthrough, we must maximize the season God has entrusted to us. We must become good stewards of the moment.

"I returned, and saw under the sun, that the race is not to the swift, nor the battle to the strong… but time and chance happeneth to them all."
Ecclesiastes 9:11 (KJV)

This passage reminds us that success is not solely determined by ability, strength, or intellect, but by discernment of timing and opportunity. You and I each have a season of opportunity. In God's eternal framework, there are windows, divinely appointed openings where eternity intersects with time.

God promised that if we would honor Him with obedience, seed, and sacrifice, He would open the windows of heaven and pour out blessing. But blessing requires capacity, and capacity requires stewardship. Windows are openings in heaven that connect eternity with time. Everyone will receive a window, a season of opportunity. What you do with that window rests squarely on your shoulders. So, the question becomes: How do we steward the season well?

Let me share three things we must be doing in this season if we are going to maximize our window.

Build

Before anything is launched or expanded, it must be built properly. Building begins with foundation. The principles of God's Word must be the cornerstone of everything we do. That foundation is made of God's wisdom, truth, and revelation. Whether you are building a business, a family, a ministry, or your personal life, it must be built on truth.

Once the foundation is secure, you are ready to build with the purpose God planted within you.

"And the rain descended, and the floods came, and the winds blew… and it fell not: for it was founded upon a rock."
Matthew 7:25 (KJV)

Building also requires counting the cost. It demands planning, preparation, and intentionality.

"For which of you, intending to build a tower, sitteth not down first, and counteth the cost…?"
Luke 14:28 (KJV)

Stewardship in this season means evaluating your resources, strengthening your relationships, and ensuring you are positioned to finish what God has assigned you to build.

Launch

Let this season become your springboard to greatness. Launching is the leap of faith. It is stepping into the deep and moving forward without fear, trusting the word God has spoken over your life.

"Launch out into the deep, and let down your nets for a draught."
Luke 5:4 (KJV)

Peter's response reveals the tension we often feel:

"Master, we have toiled all the night, and have taken nothing: nevertheless at thy word I will let down the net."
Luke 5:5 (KJV)

From this passage, we learn three critical lessons:

- Readjust your strategy and start again
- Improve the operation
- Let down your nets—go for it

Stewarding the season means refusing to let past disappointment keep you from present obedience.

Expand

Expansion is your invitation to go farther than you ever have before. It requires you to do what you have never done and trust God beyond familiar boundaries. Expansion can feel intimidating, but it can also become your walk-on-water moment.

In Matthew 14:24–32, Peter steps out of the boat in the middle of a storm. The timing seems wrong, but when Jesus is in the middle of it, it is always the right time. Here are key takeaways from that moment:

- Peter was troubled by what he saw, yet he still moved ***(Matthew 14:26)***
- Assurance from Jesus was all the confirmation he needed ***(Matthew 14:27–28)***
- Exposure to Christ's greatness expanded Peter's faith beyond his imagination ***(Matthew14:28)***

- Focus kept Peter afloat; Jesus would not let him sink!

No matter what is happening around you, stay focused. Jesus has your back.

This is your season.

This is your window.

Steward it well.

Build with wisdom.

Launch with faith.

Expand with courage.

And watch God do what only He can do.

CHAPTER 8

Passionately Pursue God's Purpose for Your Life

PURPOSE IS NOT SIMPLE, AND IT IS never confined to a single moment, achievement, or season. Purpose is complex. It cannot be fully explained or revealed in one event. Rather, purpose is what God knows about us in totality, yet He releases it through us progressively, season by season, step by step.

God always begins with the end in mind.

> *"For I know the plans and thoughts that I have for you," says the Lord, "plans for peace and well-being and not for disaster, to give you a future and a hope."*
> *Jeremiah 29:11 (AMP)*

This scripture reminds us that before we ever questioned our direction, God had already determined our destination. Purpose is not discovered by accident; it is revealed by alignment. God sees the finished picture even while we are still becoming.

Purpose burns in the depths of your soul. It is placed there by God Himself. It is the thing you cannot shake, the holy unrest that refuses to let you settle for less than what Heaven has declared over your life. Purpose creates movement. It stirs you when comfort would rather keep you still. When purpose is ignited within you, it compels you to pursue the very thing God, in His infinite wisdom, planted inside of you long before you recognized it.

Purpose is persistent.

Purpose is demanding.

Purpose is alive.

Do not allow a single moment, whether failure or success, to define who you are. Your life is not summed up by one season. Scripture reminds us that all things are working together for your good, not to confuse you, but to unveil the ultimate purpose God has designed for your life. Some seasons refine you. Some seasons stretch you. Some seasons reveal you. Each one plays a role.

With all the spiritual fire within me, I say this to you: pursue it. Chase purpose with passion. Go beyond the invisible limits that once tried to confine you. Refuse to shrink back. Refuse to settle.

This is not the time to hesitate.

This is not the time to retreat.

This is your moment to go after what God placed in you.

Go beyond the limits.

Break through the ceiling.

Crash the Glass.

PERSONAL REFLECTION MOMENTS

Chapter 1: Crash The Glass

1. What invisible barriers have I accepted as "just the way it is"?

2. When did I first begin to believe these limitations?

3. Who or what has influenced my thinking about what I can or cannot do?

4. What would my life look like if these limits no longer existed?

5. What step is God asking me to take to break through today?

____

____

____

____

____

____

____

____

____

Chapter 2: Crashing The Limits of Time

1. Where do I feel behind, delayed, or late in life?

2. How have I allowed time, age, or missed opportunities to discourage me?

3. What promises from God am I struggling to believe because of timing?

4. How does trusting God's timing change my perspective?

5. What would it look like to fully surrender my timeline to God?

____

____

____

____

____

____

____

____

Chapter 3: Don't Lose it in the Moment

1. What situations tend to trigger emotional or impulsive responses from me?

2. How have past moments of pressure affected my decisions?

3. What have I lost by reacting instead of responding in faith?

4. What has God already equipped me with for difficult moments?

5. How can I remain grounded and faithful when emotions run high?

____

____

____

____

____

____

____

____

Chapter 4: What is This Season Revealing in You?

1. What patterns, habits, or attitudes have surfaced in this season?

2. What is this season exposing that I may have ignored before?

3. How has this season stretched my faith?

4. What strengths are being developed in me right now?

5. What is God teaching me about myself in this season?

____

____

____

____

____

____

____

____

Chapter 5: The Power of Recognition

1. What has God already placed in my hands that I may be overlooking?

2. Who or what do I need to recognize differently in my life?

3. How has lack of recognition limited my growth?

4. What happens when I acknowledge God's hand in my current situation?

5. How can recognition lead to greater responsibility and stewardship?

____

____

____

____

____

____

____

____

Chapter 6: Get Uncomfortable

1. What areas of my life have become too comfortable?

2. How has comfort kept me from growth or obedience?

3. What is God asking me to step into that feels uncomfortable?

4. What fears surface when I consider change?

5. How can discomfort become a tool for transformation?

Chapter 7: Steward the Season

1. How am I currently managing the season I am in?

2. What resources, relationships, or opportunities has God entrusted to me?

3. Am I fully present, or am I waiting for the "next" season?

4. What adjustments do I need to make to steward this season well?

5. How does faithfulness now prepare me for what's next?

____

____

____

____

____

____

____

____

____

Chapter 8: Passionately Pursue God's Purpose for Your Life

1. What passions has God placed inside of me?

2. Where have I allowed distractions to pull me away from purpose?

3. What would wholehearted pursuit of God look like in my daily life?

4. What sacrifices might be required to walk fully in my purpose?

5. How can I align my actions more closely with God's calling?

____

____

____

____

____

____

____

____

ABOUT THE AUTHOR

Pastor Marcel D. Fears is a dynamic and thought-provoking orator who has traveled across the country delivering life-changing messages of hope that challenge individuals to embrace all that God has for their lives. A visionary leader, educator, entrepreneur, and bridge-builder, he is passionate about transformation and practical faith.

He is the Founder and Pastor of Overcomer's Life Church, a Christ-centered, discipleship-focused ministry in the Chicagoland area committed to being a safe-haven where lives are transformed through the power of Christ.

He is also the founder of Prayer Nation Worldwide and the owner of Marcel Fears Enterprises, Inc., focused on inspiring solutions, inspiring people, and changing lives. Pastor Fears has been married to Lady Venus Fears since 2005, and together they are the proud parents of two sons, David Eugene and Tyler Louis.

Other books by Pastor Marcel Fears

This is Where You Make It Happen
7 Principles to Love Again
Ignite Your Atmosphere
Ready. Set. Pray.

www.marcelfears.org

www.ingramcontent.com/pod-product-compliance
Lightning Source LLC
LaVergne TN
LVHW020657100826
845148LV00012B/2528

* 9 7 9 8 9 0 2 7 1 2 1 6 9 *